Book of Daring Deeds and Epic Creations

60 ultimate try-something-new, explore-the-world activities

Written by Sherry Kyle

ZONDERKIDZ

The Adventure Bible Book of Daring Deeds and Epic Creations
Copyright © 2018 by Zondervan
Illustrations © by Zondervan

This title is also available as a Zondervan ebook.

Requests for information should be addressed to:
Zonderkidz, *3900 Sparks Dr. SE, Grand Rapids, Michigan 49546*

ISBN 978-0-310763178

Published in association with the Books & Such Literary Management, 52
Mission Circle, Suite 122, PMB 170, Santa Rosa, California 95409-5370,
www.booksandsuch.com.

Zonderkidz is a trademark of Zondervan.

Content contributor: Sherry Kyle
Art direction: Cindy Davis
Interior illustrations: Dave Smith
Interior design: Denise Froehlich

Printed in China

18 19 20 21 22 23 24 /DSC/ 15 14 13 12 11 10 9 8 7 6 5 4 3 2 1

Contents

Welcome to Adventure!

The Adventure Bible Book of Daring Deeds and Epic Creations is the ultimate get-your-hands-dirty, try-something-new, explore-the-world manual for kids like YOU who want to learn, create, play, and build while having a blast doing it!

This book is full of all kinds of adventures, from nature walks and camping do's and don'ts, to making secret codes and identifying leaves and animal tracks. But that's not all. Each activity has a "Think about This" section and a Bible verse to help you explore the world *and* God's Word too!

Some of the activities require an adult's help, so make sure to ask a parent or grown-up when you come across an activity that mentions a safety warning.

But don't worry—there are plenty of activities you can do on your own! From easy, do-it-yourself crafts to fun outdoor activities, this book will show you how to find adventure indoors and out.

Ready to get started? Let the fun begin!

Aluminum Foil Art

Did you know aluminum foil can be used to sharpen dull scissors, fix loose batteries, and keep critters out of your garden? Aluminum foil can do many other things, too, including help create this picture.

What you need:

Aluminum foil
Pencil
Permanent markers
Recycled cardboard

Scissors
Scotch tape
Tacky glue

What you do:

1. Cut a piece of cardboard whatever size you like.
2. Draw a simple picture on the cardboard, such as a boat, butterfly, flower, or a geometric design.
3. Carefully go over all the lines of your drawing with a heavy line of Tacky glue. Allow time to dry.
4. Cover your picture and the piece of cardboard completely with aluminum foil. Fold around the edges and tape the aluminum foil to the back of the cardboard.
5. Gently rub the aluminum foil to expose your picture. Cool, huh?
6. Color your picture with permanent markers.

Think about This

Placing the aluminum foil on top of your glue drawing creates an impression of what is inside. God wants to make an impression on you, too, so that you will be holy in the way you live and think.

Read I Peter 1:15–16

But just as he who called you is holy, so be holy in all you do; for it is written: "Be holy, because I am holy."

Awesome Trail Mix

Surprise your friends by making this snack for your next hiking adventure.

What you need:

2 cups salted peanuts

1 cup whole pecans

1 cup pumpkin or sunflower seeds

1 cup dried cranberries or other dried fruit

1 cup M&Ms

What you do:

1. Warning: If you or your friends have nut allergies, please DO NOT make this recipe! Have a parent help you look for a nut-free version of a similar recipe.

2. Mix all the ingredients in a large plastic zipper bag. That's it!
3. You can substitute other nuts or dried fruit, depending on what you like.
4. Here's why it is good for you:
   - The salt from the nuts will replace the salt your body loses when you sweat on your hike.
   - The nuts also give you lots of nutrition and energy to keep your body moving!
   - The pumpkin or sunflower seeds provide energy and add extra crunch and flavor.
   - The sugar in dried fruit and the chocolate pieces fuel your body and your brain. And it tastes great too!

Think about This

Just as you are supplying a snack for your friends, God provides for you!

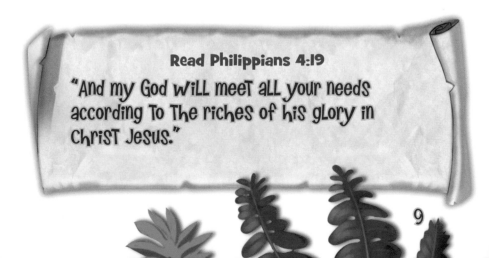

Read Philippians 4:19

"And my God will meet all your needs according to the riches of his glory in Christ Jesus."

9

Balloon Rocket

Fun facts:

- The Chinese invented the first rocket around the year 1200 AD.
- The first rockets were used for fireworks and for rescuing people at sea.
- A typical space rocket produces around a million pounds of thrust, travels around 22,000 miles per hour, and can carry 6,000 pounds!
- The most powerful rocket ever built was the Saturn V rocket, which launched the Apollo mission to the moon.
- Rockets are used to blast the space shuttle into orbit.

Build a balloon rocket by following these steps.

What you need:

Balloon	Drinking straw
2 chairs	String—6 to 8 feet
Scissors	Masking tape

What you do:

1. Thread a drinking straw on the string.
2. Tie each end of the string to two large objects, like dining room chairs or trees.
3. Place two 3-inch pieces of masking tape horizontally over the straw. Don't let the tape stick together!
4. Blow up a balloon. Pinch the end shut with your fingers instead of tying off the end.
5. Without letting air escape, carefully attach the balloon to the straw with the masking tape, then pull the balloon toward the chair or tree on the side of the opening of the balloon.
6. Now let go and watch your rocket fly along the string!

Think about This

Just as the balloon rocket thrusts into action when you let go, you can show God's love to others through your actions.

7. Why this works: action and reaction
   - Forces work in pairs. If an object moves one way, a force has to work in the opposite direction. Since the balloon is full of air, letting go of the balloon causes air to rush out of the opening creating a pushing force in the opposite direction. Cool, huh?

Read I John 3:18

"Dear children, Let us not Love with words or speech but with actions and in Truth."

Bottle Bowling

Did you know the first bowling balls were made of wood? Plastic balls with bright, swirly designs and colors were introduced around 1960. Create your own pins and bowl in your backyard with this fun activity.

What you need:

10 plastic bottles
Dish soap
White acrylic paint
Red permanent marker
Sand or small pebbles

Ball
Masking tape
Pencil
Paper

To create the pins:

1. Wash out the empty plastic bottles with dish soap. Allow time to dry.
2. Squirt a small amount of white acrylic paint into the plastic bottles until it fills each base.
3. Place the caps on the plastic bottles and tighten securely.
4. Shake the bottles to create a solid white color.
5. Remove the caps and let the paint dry overnight.
6. Draw two red stripes around the plastic bottles with the red permanent marker.
7. Add an inch of sand or small pebbles inside the bottles for weight, then return the caps.

Set the pins up in a triangle shape:

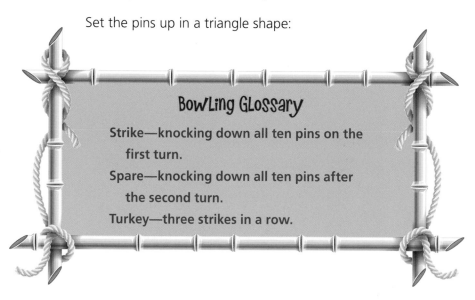

Bowling Glossary

Strike—knocking down all ten pins on the first turn.

Spare—knocking down all ten pins after the second turn.

Turkey—three strikes in a row.

How you play:

1. Make a line with masking tape about five steps (around ten feet) from the pins. Stand behind the line.
2. Lean down and roll the ball toward the front pin, trying to knock down as many pins as you can. Two tries per turn.
3. To keep score, add 1 point for each pin you knock down.
4. The first to reach 50 points wins.

Think about This

When life knocks you down, Jesus is there to pick you up.

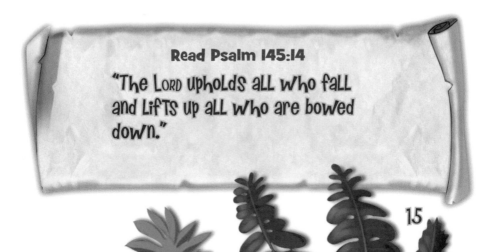

Read Psalm 145:14

"The LORD upholds all who fall and lifts up all who are bowed down."

Balloon Tennis

Even if you can't find a partner, you can play balloon tennis. Grab a "racket" in each hand and get ready to have fun!

What you need:

Balloons	Markers
Duct tape	Paper plates
Glue	Craft sticks

What you do:

1. Glue a paper plate to the end of a craft stick to form your tennis racket. If you have a real tennis racquet or ping-pong paddle, you can use that instead.
2. With markers, draw racket strings on the paper plate.

3. Wrap the end of the craft stick with duct tape for a firm grip.

4. Blow up balloons for tennis balls.

5. Find a friend to play with and make up your own rules, or follow these:

- The player who keeps the balloon up in the air without touching the ground wins a point, just like tennis. First player to reach 10 points wins.

- As you hit the ball back and forth, each player calls out a target for the next player to hit, such as a chair, coffee table, or a door, if indoors. (Note: make sure all fragile items are put away.) First player to reach 5 points wins.

- Each player counts how many times he can hit the balloon in the air without letting it touch the ground. The player with the highest number wins.

Read Hebrews 12:1b–2

"And let us run with perseverance the race marked out for us, fixing our eyes on Jesus, the pioneer and perfecter of faith."

Build Your Own Bird Feeder

Fun facts:

- There are 10,000 species of birds worldwide.
- Birds have feathers, lay eggs, and are warm-blooded.
- Birds have hollow bones, which help them fly.

Create this one-of-a-kind bird feeder for the birds in your neighborhood!

What you need:

Empty half-gallon milk carton (the cardboard kind, not the plastic kind)
Permanent marker
Ruler
Scissors or a craft knife
Paint, in your favorite color
Dish soap
Paintbrush
Hole punch
Craft sticks
Tacky glue
Yarn or twine
Birdseed

What you do:

1. Rinse the milk carton with water. Set aside to dry.

2. Draw a large square on the front and back of the milk carton three inches up from the bottom of the carton.

3. With the help of an adult, cut out the squares with scissors or a craft knife.

4. Mix paint with a small amount of dish soap to keep the paint from peeling. Decorate your bird feeder with the paint. Allow time to dry.

> ### Think about This
> Just as you are helping to take care of the birds, God takes care of you!

5. Punch a hole below the square opening on each side.

6. Insert craft sticks in the holes so the birds can sit on a perch. Use craft glue, such as Tacky glue, to help the sticks stay in place.

7. Punch a hole in the top of the milk carton. Thread a piece of yarn or twine through to use as a hanger.

8. Fill the bird feeder with birdseed.

9. Hang your bird feeder on a tree 6 feet down from the lowest branch to keep the birds safe from predators, such as squirrels and cats.

10. Be patient. It may take up to two weeks for the birds to discover your bird feeder.

"Look at the birds of the air; they do not sow or reap or store away in barns, and yet your heavenly Father feeds them. Are you not much more valuable than they?"

Coded Secret Message

The word "alphabet" comes from the first two letters of the Greek alphabet, "alpha" and "beta."

Fun facts:

- Before the Greek alphabet, people drew pictures to get their point across.
- Over the years, the drawings became symbols. But there were too many symbols to remember them all, so the symbols became letters.
- The Phoenicians taught the Greeks about writing and the alphabet.
- The Greeks added vowels and decided how each letter should be pronounced.
- The Greek alphabet was originally read and written from right to left and used only capital letters.

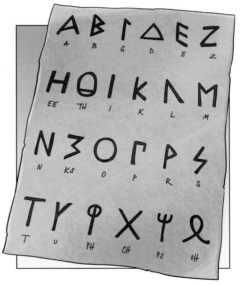

What you need:

Paper

Pencil

White construction paper

White crayon

Watercolor paints and

    paintbrush

Newspaper

What you do:

1. To create a coded secret message, use the Greek alphabet, or try one of these secret codes:
2. Write the message backwards.
3. Example: GOD IS GOOD = DOOG SI DOG
4. Numbers stand for letters based on each letter's place in the alphabet. A = 1, B = 2, C = 3, and so forth. Example: LOVE IS PATIENT = 12 15 22 5 9 19 16 1 20 9 5 14 20
5. Invisible secret code. Write a message on a white piece of construction paper using a white crayon. The person receiving the message paints over the message using watercolor paint to reveal what was written.
6. Create your own secret code using pictures or symbols to match the letters, such as shapes, arrows, hearts, or flowers.

Read Proverbs 2:1, 4–5

"If you accepT my words and sTore up my commands wiThin you . . . and if you Look for iT as for siLver and search for iT as for hidden Treasure, Then you wiLL undersTand The fear of The Lord and find The knowLedge of God."

23

Cloud Soap

Soap comes in many forms, such as a bar and liquid—or transformed into a fluffy-looking cloud! Change a bar of Ivory soap into a white cloud, and then back into a bar again with this amazing activity.

What you need:

Bar of Ivory soap (only this brand works for this activity)
Food coloring
Paper towel
Microwave
Rubber gloves
Wooden spoon or electric mixer

What you do:

1. Place a paper towel inside your microwave. Set the bar of Ivory soap on top. Press two minutes on your microwave timer and start. Watch the soap grow and turn into a cloud! Cool, huh? If the soap stops growing, stop your microwave before the two minutes are up.

2. To change it back into a bar again, break the cloud apart into a bowl.

3. With a parent's help, stir with a wooden spoon or electric mixer and add warm water, just until the soap comes together. To see if it's ready, grab some in your hand to see if it sticks together. Add a few drops of food coloring to create colored soap.

Think about This

When you ask Jesus into your heart, he washes away your sin and transforms you through the gift of the Holy Spirit and his Word, the Bible.

4. Wearing rubber gloves, mold your soap by hand into whatever shape you'd like.

5. Let the soap dry for a few days.

6. Take a bath or shower with your new soap. Enjoy!

Read Psalm 51:10

"Create in me a pure heart, O God, and renew a steadfast spirit within me."

25

Cosmic Art

Try this out-of-this-world activity to create a stellar work of art.

What you need:

Food coloring—different colors
Plastic lid (from butter, hummus, sour cream, yogurt, etc.)
Toothpicks
White glue

What you do:

1. Cover the entire inside surface of the plastic lid with a generous amount of white glue.
2. Put a drop or two of each food coloring at different places on the glue.

3. Swirl the colors around with a toothpick, being careful not to combine too many colors or else they will turn brown.
4. As you swirl the colors, notice how your art starts to look like a colorful nebula!
5. Let dry for a few days.
6. Hang your cosmic art in your room or give it as a gift.

Think about This

A galaxy is a huge collection of gas, dust, and billions of stars and their solar systems. The God who made the galaxies is also the God who made you.

Read Psalm 8:3-4

"When I consider your heavens, the work of your fingers, the moon and the stars, which you have set in place, what is mankind that you are mindful of them, human beings that you care for them?"

Craft Stick and Paper Fish

During Bible times, cooked fish was a big part of the Galilean diet. Do you like to eat fish? Even if you don't, you'll have fun creating this craft stick and paper fish.

What you need:

4 craft sticks—colored or natural wood
Markers
Acrylic paint
Paintbrush
Tacky glue
Construction paper
Scissors
Wiggle eyes

What you do:

1. Glue the craft sticks together in the shape of a fish. Start by making a V with two Popsicle sticks and glue together. Make an X with two other craft sticks and glue together.

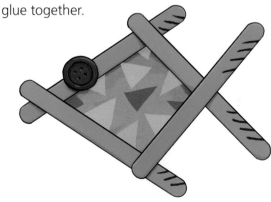

2. Once dry, turn the V on its side so that the opening is to the right. Glue the X an inch down the opening of the V, leaving room for the fins.

3. Once the glue is dry, color the craft stick fish your favorite color with markers or acrylic paint.

4. Next, draw a fun pattern on the construction paper with markers. Be creative!

5. Glue the fish on the paper and cut away the excess.

Think about This

One day, the disciples went fishing and didn't catch a single fish. When Jesus spoke, the disciples pulled in 153 fish! (John 21) Just as Jesus performed a miracle for the disciples, he can do a miracle for you.

6. Put a dab of glue on the back of a wiggle eye and attach it to the fish, or draw an eye with a marker.

7. Optional: Add glitter, buttons, sequins, or anything else that gives your fish personality!

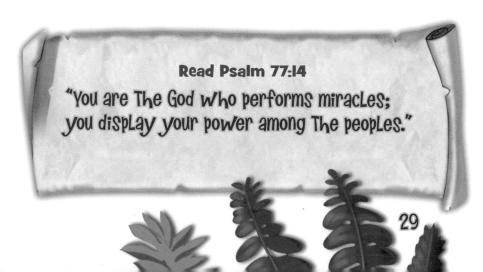

Read Psalm 77:14

"You are The God who performs miracles; you display your power among The peoples."

Cross with Sticks and Twine

Next time you're on a nature walk, grab a couple of small sticks and create this project.

What you need:

Two sticks (this works best if you can find one stick that is about half as long as the other stick)
1 to 2 feet of twine
Scissors

What you do:

1. With your left index finger and thumb, hold the sticks in the shape of a cross, with the shorter stick on top.
2. Place the twine diagonally behind the crossed sticks, leaving several inches on the upper left to tie in a knot at the end.

3. Wrap the long end of the twine around the sticks diagonally four times in the same direction, then wrap it around the opposite way four times.

4. Knot the ends together and cut the remaining twine.

Read John 3:16

"For God so loved the world that he gave his one and only Son, that whoever believes in him shall not perish but have eternal life."

31

David's Slingshot

The Bible says David killed Goliath with just one stone from his slingshot. Here's your chance to create a slingshot like David used.

What you need:

2 30-inch shoestrings
Old sock

Scissors
Small, foam ball, like a Nerf ball

What you do:

1. A slingshot is a weapon, which means you must be very careful how and where you use it. Ask a parent to supervise before beginning this activity.
2. Cut a rectangle from an old sock 3 inches long and 1½ inches wide.
3. Fold the cloth in half lengthwise. Cut two small holes, one on each end, and thread the tips of the shoestrings through the holes and tie knots to hold in place.

4. On the far end of one of the shoestrings, tie a small loop. This slips over the middle finger of your throwing hand.

5. To create the launching string, hold both shoestrings in your hand, keeping the pocket level, and tie a knot a few inches down the shoestring where your thumb and index finger meet.

6. Place a small, foam ball into the pocket.

7. To launch, hold the pocket level. Gently swing in a circular movement and release the knot when your arm is straight down. If the ball does not shoot straight, adjust the timing of the release.

8. Remember: Do not point the slingshot at animals or people!

Think about This

In Bible times, shepherds used slings to protect their flocks. You are one of God's sheep, and he will protect you.

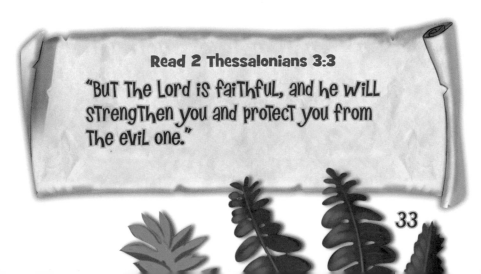

Read 2 Thessalonians 3:3

"But the Lord is faithful, and he will strengthen you and protect you from the evil one."

Duct Tape Nature Journal

Writing or doodling in a nature journal is a lot of fun. You can collect bits of nature, like leaves or flowers, and jot down what you see and observe. Go on, try it!

What you need:

Ruler
Recycled cardboard
Scissors
Duct tape in your favorite color
Construction paper
Glue
Paper (plain or lined)
Hole punch
Twine (about 2 feet)
Markers, pens, or
    pencils for writing

What you do:

1. Measure and cut two 8.5 x 11" pieces of recycled cardboard for the front and back of your journal.
2. Wrap the colorful duct tape around the front and back pieces of cardboard, similar to a book cover.
3. Create a design, such as flowers or a tree, on the front cover with construction paper. Glue on the pieces.
4. Use plain white paper or lined notebook paper for the inside pages.
5. Punch three evenly spaced holes through the front and back covers, as well as through the paper, making sure the holes line up.
6. Thread the twine through each of the holes twice, then tie in a knot at the top to secure.
7. Go outside and journal your next big adventure.

Think abouT This

You can talk to God by writing in your journal. Thank him for his wonderful creation.

Read Revelations 4:11

"You are worThy, our Lord and God, To receive glory and honor and power, for you creaTed all Things, and by your will They were creaTed and have Their being."

Finger Knitting

Finger knitting is a surefire way to create a scarf in a jiffy! You can finger knit on a road trip, while watching TV, or when you need to relax.

What you need:

Scissors
Yarn
Your hands

What you do:

1. Hold the palm of your hand toward you and secure the end of your yarn between your thumb and index finger. The tail should be a couple of inches long and resting in your palm.
2. Wrap the yarn behind your index finger, in front of your middle finger, behind the ring finger, and in front of your pinky finger.
3. Continue wrapping the yarn around the back of your pinky finger, in front of your ring finger, behind the middle finger, and in front of your index finger. Make sure you don't make the yarn too tight.
4. Repeat steps 2 and 3.
5. You should now have two rows of yarn on your fingers. Pull the bottom row of loops over the tops of

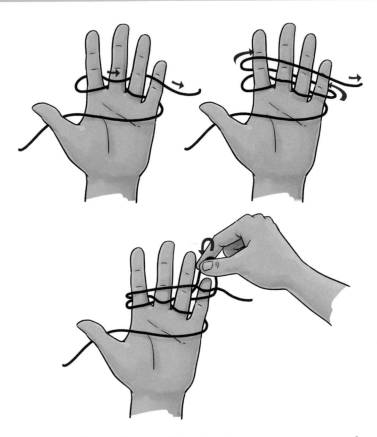

each of your fingers. You should now see one row of yarn on your fingers.

6. Lay the long strand of yarn across your fingers, just above the row of loops on your fingers. Once again, take the bottom row of yarn over the top of all four fingers, starting with the index finger and working your way across to the pinky finger.

7. Repeat this process; however, the long strand of yarn will now be on your right. Lay the yarn across your

fingers, and start with the pinky finger this time, looping the bottom row over the top of your finger. Do this with all four fingers.

8. Repeat steps 6 and 7 until you are happy with the length of your scarf.

9. To finish, take the loop on your index finger and move it to the middle finger, so that you now have two loops on your middle finger. Take the bottom loop over the top of your middle finger.

10. Take the remaining loop on your middle finger and move it to the next finger. Once again, take the bottom loop over the top of your finger.

11. Move the remaining loop on that finger to your pinky finger. Once again, take the bottom loop over the top of your finger. You should now have only one remaining loop.

> ### Think about This
>
> **Just as you knit a strand of yarn, God made you and knit you together.**

12. Cut the long end of the yarn a few inches from your hand to create a tail.

13. Carefully remove the loop from your pinky finger, and tuck the tail through the remaining loop and pull tight.

Read Psalm 139:13–14

"For you created my inmost being; you knit me together in my mother's womb. I praise you because I am fearfully and wonderfully made; your works are wonderful, I know that full well."

Flower Press

You can keep fresh flowers a very long time when they are dried and pressed. The more colorful the flower, the prettier it will be. Try it!

What you need:

Flowers   Printer paper

Scissors   3 or 4 heavy books

What you do:

1. Choose flowers that have freshly bloomed. Make sure you get permission to pick them.
2. Prep your flowers by cutting the stems at an angle and removing the lower leaves.

3. If you have chosen to press thick flowers, such as roses, remove half of the petals by cutting straight down the middle. This will make the flower easier to press.

4. Dry the flowers on printer paper. Do not use paper towels as they may leave a mark on the petals.

5. Find a heavy book to press your flowers. The pages may get wet and wrinkled, so choose one you don't mind ruining.

6. Place a flower between two pieces of printer paper and stick it in the middle of the book. If you are pressing more than one flower, space them evenly throughout the book.

Think about This

Flowers fade away, but the Word of God lasts forever!

7. Stack more books on top to add weight.

8. Every few days, carefully change the printer paper so that mold does not form. The flowers should be dry in two to three weeks. Remove the dried flowers very carefully, and place them someplace safe, like in a picture frame.

Read Isaiah 40:8

"The grass withers and the flowers fall, but the word of our God endures forever."

Fruit of the Spirit

Fun fruit facts:

- The most popular fruit is the tomato.
- There are over 1,000 different kinds of apples.
- Strawberries have more vitamin C than oranges.

Draw a picture of your favorite fruit by following these steps.

What you need:

Piece of fruit
Paper
Pencil
Eraser
Black pen
Colored pencils

What you do:

1. Choose a piece of fruit to draw.
2. With a pencil, start by drawing the main shape. An apple or orange has a circular shape. A banana is long and narrow, while a pear is oval on the top and more circular on the bottom.

3. Look at your fruit more closely and begin to make small changes to the shape on your paper to look more like the individual piece of fruit.

4. Add more details. Draw the stem and peel, and anything else you see that makes your drawing look real.

5. Use a fine-tip pen to add dimension.

6. Erase any pencil lines.

7. Color in the fruit with colored pencils. Shade in any areas that appear darker.

8. Step back and admire your artwork while you eat your fruit!

Think abouT This

The Bible talks about a different kind of fruit—the fruit of the Spirit. When we ask Jesus into our hearts, the Holy Spirit fills us with God's love.

Read Galatians 5: 22–23

"BuT The fruiT of The SpiriT is Love, joy, peace, forbearance, kindness, goodness, faiThfulness, genTLeness, and self-conTroL. AgainsT such Things There is no Law."

Geocaching

Want to hunt for treasure? Geocaching might be for you! Discover treasure, or "caches" containing small trinkets or inexpensive toys hidden all over the world.

What you need:

Computer

A handheld GPS or a
    smartphone

Backpack or treasure box to
    hold your supplies

Small toys

Comfortable shoes

Water bottles

Snacks

What you do:

1. With parental supervision, go to Geocaching.com and create a free account.

2. Decide which geocache you want to find. For your first time, look for a "one-star" rating for ease of terrain. You may need to hike up to a mile or two, so make sure you are wearing comfortable shoes and bring a water bottle and snacks in your backpack.

3. The rule of geocaching is if you take something from the cache, you must replace it with something of the same value. If you want to exchange treasure, look for regular or larger-size caches.

4. Head out on your adventure with a parent or friend. Use your GPS to guide you to the exact location of the cache.

5. When you are within 15–20 feet of the cache, begin to look around. You may find it in hollow logs, tied to objects, or under bushes. The possibilities are endless.

Think about This

Seeking God is like searching for treasure. All you need to do is ask in the name of Jesus, and he will answer your prayers according to his will.

6. Once you find it, open up the cache and discover what's inside. Feel free to exchange a toy for one of your own.

7. If there is a logbook in the cache, write the date and

sign your name. (Otherwise, log your visit on your computer once you get home.)

8. If for some reason you can't find the cache, don't despair! Sometimes people forget to put them back or rain washes them away. The best thing to do is to contact the original hider and let them know. You may have been looking in the wrong location, and the hider can give you a clue.

9. Optional: Buy the Geocaching app for your smart-phone with parental permission. You can log your adventures right on your phone!

Read Matthew 7:8

"For everyone who asks, receives; The one who seeks finds; and To The one who knocks, The door will be opened."

Green Camping

"Going green" doesn't mean you have to dress up like a leprechaun! Green living is taking care of the environment. Practice this by keeping your campsite green and clean.

What you need:

Camp chairs
Tarp
Mat
Hand broom and dustpan
Paper towel holder and paper towels
Pop-up hamper
  with zipper
Trash bags
Large plastic bin
  with lid
Water jug with
  spigot
Dish soap
Sponge
Hand towels

What you do:

1. Plan ahead! Only bring what you are going to use while camping and leave the rest at home.
2. Only camp in areas marked for your campsite so that you don't disturb natural habitat.
3. Place a mat by the door and wipe your feet before going inside your tent.
4. Keep a hand broom and dustpan inside your tent for easy clean up.
5. For safety, set up camp chairs in open areas a good distance from the fire pit.
6. During the day, set the paper towel holder on the picnic table and take only what you need.
7. Place a trash bag inside a pop-up hamper with a zipper as a garbage can to keep animals out. If the campsite doesn't have a large trash bin, bring your trash home and throw it away there. Check the campsite's rules for trash. Some have lockers to keep the bears away.
8. Bring reusable plates, silverware, and cups.
9. Scrape leftover food into a container to compost later.

Think abouT This

Everything on the earth belongs to God, including water, plants, and animals. You can show God how much you love him by taking care of his creation.

10. Use a large bin as a sink to wash your dishes—or your hands and face. Rinse with water from a water jug that has a spigot and dry with a hand towel.

11. During the night, store food in a bin (with the lid closed tight) and put it in the car. Make sure the windows are closed to keep animals, like bears, away.

12. Remember to pick up after your pet!

13. Before going home, make sure your fire is out and completely cold.

14. Take one last look around your campsite for small pieces of trash and pick them up, even if it's not yours. Be a good steward by leaving the campsite cleaner than you found it!

Read Psalm 24:1

"The earth is the Lord's, and everything in it, the world, and all who live in it."

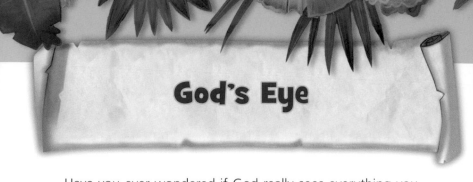

God's Eye

Have you ever wondered if God really sees everything you do? Well, the answer is yes, he does! Consider this truth as you make this cool project.

What you need:

Craft sticks or small twigs
Scissors
Tacky glue
Yarn—four colors, both light and dark (or use a variegated yarn that has many colors)

What you do:

1. Find twigs that are 6 to 8 inches in length or use two craft sticks. If you are using twigs, make sure they are strong and you remove loose bark.
2. Glue the twigs or craft sticks together in the shape of a cross. Let dry.
3. Take one color yarn and allow a three-inch tail in the back of your cross before you start wrapping.

4. To wrap, bring the yarn across the top stick and wrap around, then go clockwise across the next stick and wrap around.

5. Keep going to the next stick, across the top and wrapping around, and so forth until you have gone around at least four more times to create the *eye*. Catch the tail as you go, to hold the yarn in place.

6. To add a color, tie the ends of the two colors together in a tight knot and keep wrapping. Decide how thick you want each color to be before adding another color.

7. Finish the God's Eye by gluing the tip of the final yarn to the back of the cross. Tie a small loop of yarn for a hanger.

8. Optional: Add decorations, such as beads, feathers, or a fun tassel.

> ### Think abouT This
> The Bible says God watches over you and will show you which way to go.

Read Psalm 32:8

"I wiLL insTrucT you and Teach you in The way you shouLd go: I wiLL counseL you wiTh my LoVing eye on you."

Hand Prayer

Saying a prayer shouldn't feel like a chore. God wants you to spend time with him. Use this activity to help you find the words to pray.

What you need:

Paper
Colored markers

What you do:

1. Place your hand on a piece of paper with your fingers spread out slightly and draw around it with a black marker.
2. Pray this prayer:
3. On the drawing, write the word PRAISE and Psalm 92:1 with a purple marker on the small pinky finger. Read the verse and praise God for being who he is.
4. Write the word THANKS and 1 Chronicles 16:34 with an orange marker on the ring finger. Read the verse and give thanks to God for all he has done in your life.

5. Write the word CONFESS and 1 John 1:9 with a red marker on the middle finger. Read the verse, and admit your sin and need for a Savior.

6. Write the word OTHERS and 1 Thessalonians 1:2 with a green marker on the index finger. Read the verse and pray for others.

7. Write the word MYSELF and Philippians 4:6 with a yellow marker on the thumb. Read the verse and pray for yourself.

8. Write the word LISTEN and Proverbs 19:20 with a blue marker on the palm. Read the verse and spend time listening to what God is telling you.

Think about This

You don't have to use fancy words when you pray. Talk to God like you talk to a parent or a friend.

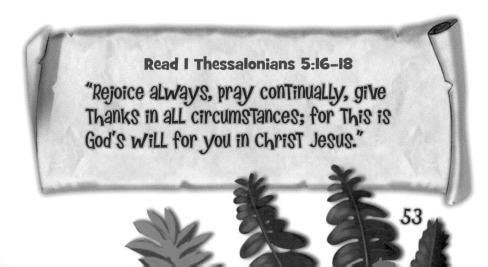

Read 1 Thessalonians 5:16–18

"Rejoice always, pray continually, give Thanks in all circumstances; for this is God's will for you in Christ Jesus."

Hiking Essentials Pack

Today is a great day to lace up those hiking boots and explore God's amazing creation! Before you go, make sure you have everything you need for a safe hike, including a hiking partner, and tell someone where you are going and when you'll be back. If you have a cell phone, take one with you.

What you need:

Comfortable backpack or hiking bag
Map and compass
Sunglasses and sunscreen
Extra clothing,
   including a hat
Flashlight
First-aid supplies
Waterproof matches,
   lighter
Knife and duct tape
   for unexpected
   repairs
Extra snacks and food
Water

Emergency shelter, such as a light tarp, or even a large
   plastic trash bag

Other important things to bring when taking a long hike:

1. An adult and two friends, in case someone gets hurt. One person can stay with the injured person, and the others can go for help.
2. Knowledge of the area you are hiking
3. Cell phone
4. Insect repellent
5. Whistle
6. Small mirror

Think about This

When hiking, it is important to be prepared in case of an emergency. It's just as important to be ready to give an answer to people when they ask about Jesus!

Read I Peter 3:15

"But in your hearts revere Christ as Lord. Always be prepared to give an answer to everyone who asks you to give the reason for the hope that you have. But do this with gentleness and respect."

Homemade Rock Candy

Rock candy has been around for over a thousand years. Surprisingly, it was used as medicine before it became a popular treat. And guess what? You can make it at home.

What you need:

1 cup water

3 cups white granulated sugar

Bag clips

Small packets of powdered drink mix

Large glass measuring cup

3 wooden craft sticks

Saucepan

Spoon

Plate

3 small mason jars or glasses

Butter knife

What you do:

1. Bring water to a boil.
2. Add 1 cup of sugar and stir until dissolved. Do this two more times, for a total of 3 cups of sugar. Set aside to cool for 15 minutes.
3. Pour a small amount of sugar on a plate. Dip half of the craft sticks in water, then roll in the sugar. Let them dry.
4. Pour a small packet of drink mix into each mason jar. This will give the rock candy a fun flavor and bright color.
5. Ask a parent to transfer the hot sugar water into a large glass measuring cup, so that you can easily pour equal amounts of the liquid into the mason jars or glasses. Stir each one more time.

> ### Think about This
> Did you know the Bible says God is a rock of refuge? We don't need to worry because we are safe when we trust in him.

6. Put a craft stick in the center of each of the mason jars, without touching the bottom, and use a bag clip so the craft sticks stay in place and sugar crystals can form.
7. Let the rock candy grow between seven days and two weeks! You'll need lots of patience for this step.
8. To take the rock candy out, first remove the clips, then

take a butter knife and tap on the surface of the rock candy by going along the edge. Dump out the excess liquid. If you are having a difficult time getting the craft stick out, run the outside of the mason jar under hot water from your kitchen faucet. Gently pry the craft stick loose and enjoy! Share the other two rock candy sticks with friends.

Read Psalm 71:3

"Be my rock of refuge, To which I can always go; give The command To save me, for you are my rock and my forTress."

How to Build a Fire

What's a camping trip without roasted marshmallows and s'mores? But first you need a campfire! Ask a parent to help you make the perfect blaze.

What you need:

Small shovel

Lighter or matches

Tinder (dead dry plants and grasses, paper, dry leaves or needles)

Kindling (dry twigs and wood pieces or cardboard)

Fire logs no bigger than your arm

Bucket with dirt or sand to pour on the fire if you need to extinguish it

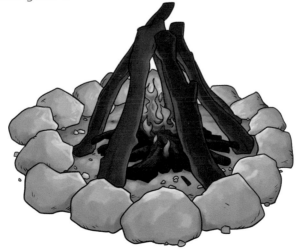

What you do:

1. IMPORTANT! Ask a parent to help you. Safety first!
2. Build a campfire in a ready-made firepit, but if one isn't available clear an area about 3 feet in diameter. Make sure it isn't too close to grass or plants that could catch fire. Line the circle with rocks and dig a pit in the center several inches deep with a small shovel.
3. Set kindling in the middle of your fire-pit, leaving some bare spaces for air circulation.
4. Place your tinder on the kindling.
5. Place firewood around your kindling, carefully arranging the logs like a tepee.
6. Have a parent light the kindling using a match or a lighter. Slowly add more kindling.
7. Blow air onto the fire to grow the heat.
8. After a while, the tepee structure will fall. Add more logs to keep the fire going.
9. Reminder: Do not burn trash! Make sure your fire is completely out and cold before leaving. Cover with dirt or sand.

> ### Think about This
>
> Fire is very powerful! The Bible tells us that the Holy Spirit came to earth as tongues of fire, resting on the heads of each apostle as they were filled with the Holy Spirit. That same Holy Spirit lives inside of you!

Read Acts 2:1–4a

"When the day of Pentecost came, they were all together in one place. Suddenly a sound like the blowing of a violent wind came from heaven and filled the whole house where they were sitting. They saw what seemed to be tongues of fire that separated and came to rest on each of them. All of them were filled with the Holy Spirit."

How to Set Up a Tent

Tents come in all shapes and sizes. Whether you're in a one-person tent or one designed for twelve, you can have a blast in your home-away-from-home.

What you need:

Tent
Plastic or vinyl tarp
Rubber mallet

What you do:

1. Find a flat, level area in a campsite. Pay attention to the direction of the wind, where the sun will rise, how close you will be to the firepit, and where the restrooms are to help you locate the best place to set up your tent.
2. Remove any rocks, twigs, or debris where your tent is going to be placed.
3. Spread a tarp on the ground.
4. Empty your tent bag and spread out the bottom part of your tent on the tarp. You want the tarp to be slightly smaller than your tent to keep the bottom of the tent dry. Decide which way you want your tent to go, and where the opening will be.

> **Think about This**
>
> When your faith is built on a firm foundation, you will be able to endure many tests and trials.

5. Connect your tent poles and put them through the flaps in the top of the tent. (Each tent is different so make sure you read the directions for your particular tent.) Most tent poles, however, form an X across the top of the tent.
6. Have a parent help you raise the tent. The tent poles will bend so that you can fit the ends into the corner hooks/loops.

7. Make sure the tent sits on the tarp, and attach the corners to the ground using metal stakes. You may need to use the rubber mallet if the ground is hard.

8. Some tents come with a rain guard to cover the top of the tent in case it starts to rain.

Read Matthew 7:24–25

"Therefore everyone who hears these words of mine and puts them into practice is like a wise man who built his house on the rock. The rain came down, the streams rose, and the winds blew and beat against that house; yet it did not fall, because it had its foundation on the rock."

Identifying Animal Tracks

Over the years, knowing how to identify animal tracks has helped people find food, watch for dangerous predators, and discover interesting facts about how animals live. By creating this mold, you can be a wildlife tracker too!

What you need:

Flour	Newspaper	Empty round
Water	Old clothes	plastic container
Mixing bowl	Rubber gloves	Scissors
Old spoon	Craft stick	

What you do:

1. Cut off the top 2 inches of an empty plastic container, such as an old sour cream or cream cheese container (or anything else that is 4–6 inches around) to form a plastic ring.
2. With a parent's permission, explore your neighborhood for animal tracks after it has rained. The ground will be wet and muddy, perfect for little critters to leave their mark.

3. Once you have discovered a track, remove any leaves, rocks, sticks, or any other debris close to the track.
4. Center the top of an empty plastic container over the track and press it slightly into the ground.
5. To make homemade plaster, pour 3 cups of flour into a mixing bowl. Add 2 cups of warm water and slowly stir until there are no lumps of flour. This will take a couple of minutes. The texture should be thick, but not difficult to stir. If it seems runny, add more flour. And if it seems too thick, add a bit of water. Tap the bowl against a hard surface to remove air bubbles.
6. Pour the mixture against the inside of the plastic ring to slowly fill the track. Add a couple more inches of plaster to create the *cast*, or the plastic mold of your animal track.
7. Allow the cast to harden. It may take an hour or more.
8. Once dry, it's time to remove the cast. With a craft stick, dig around the plastic circle, then gently lift the cast. If there is resistance, stop and continue digging in the dirt until the cast comes out easily.

Think about This

God created all the animals, and he created you too! Every day he continues to mold you into what he wants you to be.

9. Set your cast on newspaper, and carefully carry it home to dry for a few more days.

10. Once your cast is chilly to the touch, carefully wash it off with cool water.

11. Identify your track to one of these common animals:

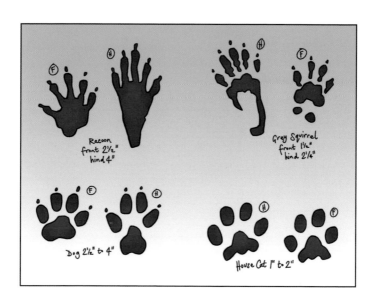

Racoon
front 2½"
hind 4"

Grey Squirrel
front 1¼"
hind 2¼"

Dog 2½" to 4"

House Cat 1" to 2"

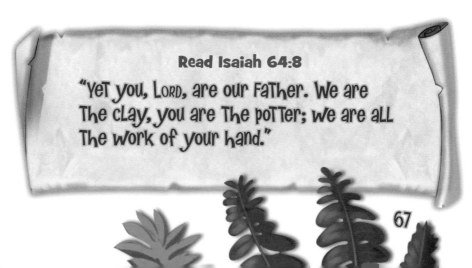

Read Isaiah 64:8

"Yet you, Lord, are our Father. We are the clay, you are the potter; we are all the work of your hand."

How to Use a Compass

A compass is a valuable tool for hikers, campers, pilots, and sea captains. Basically, everyone should know how to use a compass. It's easy!

What you need:

A compass

What you do:

1. Look at the compass. N, S, E, and W stand for the directions north, south, east, and west. These same directions are shown on a map using a symbol called the *compass rose*.

2. The red and black (or silver) arrow on a compass is called the *compass needle*. The red part of the arrow always points to the North Pole due to the earth's magnetic pull.

3. Hold the compass flat in your hand and see which way the arrow is pointing. If you'd like

> ### Think about This
> When you don't know which direction to go in your life, trust God to guide you.

to go south, you would need to go in the opposite direction. East would be to the right and left would be west.

4. That's it! If you don't have a compass, ask a parent to use a smartphone. Most smartphones come with a compass app, and you can use the app to explore the world!

Read Proverbs 3:5-6

"Trust in the Lord with all your heart and lean not on your own understanding; in all your ways submit to him, and he will make your paths straight."

Identifying Leaves

Fun facts:

- Leaves provide food for the plant.
- A leaf is an organ of the plant with two basic parts: the blade and the petiole (the part that joins the leaf to the stem).
- A simple leaf has a single blade, and a compound leaf consists of two or more separate blades, called a leaflet.
- The veins carry nutrients and water in and out of the leaves.
- Leaves come in many shapes and sizes.

During the fall months, many leaves change color and fall from the trees, but you don't have to wait for fall to identify the leaves in your neighborhood. Do it right now!

What you need:

Backpack   Snacks
Clear tape   Tacky glue
Notebook and pencil   Water bottle

What you do:

1. Go on a nature walk with a parent or a friend and find as many different types of trees and leaves as possible.
2. Gather leaves as you go. Take a picture of each tree

to print out, or draw a picture of the tree in your notebook.

3. Write down any other interesting facts, such as where the tree is located, how big the tree is, and if there are any animals living in the tree.

4. Once home, press your leaves between newspaper and lay heavy books on top.

5. Identify each leaf and write down the name in your notebook. Tape or glue the leaf next to your drawing or photo.

6. Here are some common leaves found in the United States:

ELDER ALDER HOLLY ASH BEECH HAWTHORN ROWAN

Read Deuteronomy 31:8

"The Lord himself goes before you and will be with you; he will never leave you nor forsake you. Do not be afraid; do not be discouraged."

Leaf Tracing

Parts of a leaf:

- Blade—the broad flat part of a leaf.
- Leaf veins—lines that run through the blade that carry food and water to the tree.
- Petiole—stem of the leaf.

Capture the details of fall leaves by doing this activity!

What you need:

Fall leaves
Printer paper
Crayons or colored pencils

What you do:

1. Collect fall leaves of different sizes and shapes from your neighborhood.
2. Place a leaf face down on the table.
3. Set a piece of printer paper on top.
4. Using a crayon or colored pencil, color over the top of the leaf. Watch as the details of the leaf appear.
5. After you've rubbed over the entire leaf, remove it from under the paper and try a different leaf in a new color.
6. Overlap the leaves to create a beautiful collage.
7. Optional: Trace over the leaves using different types of paper, such as wax paper, parchment paper, or aluminum foil.

> ### Think about This
>
> **Just as your drawing is an imprint of the leaf, you are created in the image of God!**

Read Genesis 1:27

"So God created mankind in his own image, in The image of God he created Them; maLe and femaLe he created Them."

73

Learn the First-Aid Basics

Knowing what to do in an emergency can save someone's life. Follow these steps to help someone in need.

Your home first-aid kit should include:

Adhesive tape

Antibiotic cream

Bandages

Cotton balls

Disposable gloves

Elastic bandage

Gauze squares

Hydrogen peroxide

Rubbing alcohol

Scissors

Liquid soap

Thermometer

Tweezers

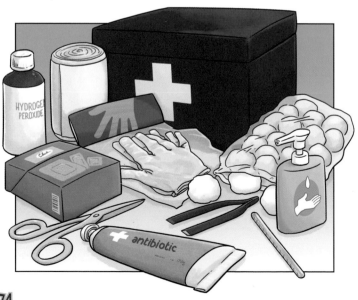

Bleeding

What to do:

1. Stop bleeding by putting pressure on the wound with a clean cloth or gauze square.
2. Gently clean the cut using soap and warm water.
3. Apply antibiotic cream to prevent an infection. Cover with a sterile bandage.
4. If a cut is large, get help from an adult or call 9–1–1.

Broken Bone

What to do:

1. Call 9–1–1.
2. Stop any bleeding by putting pressure on the wound with a clean cloth or gauze square.
3. Apply ice packs wrapped in cloth to limit swelling and relieve pain.
4. Find something to make a splint, such as sticks, boards, or rolled up newspapers. Wrap an elastic bandage around the splint and bones to prevent the injured bones from moving.
5. Lay the person down and raise their legs, then wait for help to arrive.

Burn

What to do:

1. Call 9-1-1.
2. Remove clothing from burned areas, unless it is stuck to the skin.
3. Stick the burned area under cool (not cold) water until the pain lessens. Do not to put butter, oil, or ice on the burn.
4. Apply a gauze bandage if you don't see a blister.

> ### Think about This
>
> The Bible is like a first-aid kit to help you when you are sad, hurt, or in trouble.

Nosebleed

What to do:

1. Have the person sit in a chair and tip their head slightly forward.
2. Pinch the soft part of the nose (just below the bony part) for 10 minutes.

Read Psalm 119:50

"My comfort in my suffering is This: Your promise preserves my Life."

Major Constellations

A constellation is a group of visible stars that form a pattern in the night sky. The pattern may take the form of an animal, a mythical creature, a person, or an inanimate object, such as a microscope or a crown.

Fun facts:

- There are 88 official constellations.
- Some constellations are visible in the northern hemisphere, and others are visible in the southern hemisphere.
- Constellations that can be seen in both hemispheres appear upside down in the southern hemisphere.
- Most constellations can only be seen at certain times of the year.
- Only a few constellations can be seen all year long.
- The sun is the only known star in our galaxy not part of a constellation.

What you need:

Small marshmallows
Toothpicks
Cardboard or other flat surface
Book of constellations

What you do:

1. Re-create these famous constellations using toothpicks to connect the marshmallow stars. Lay flat to see.

   Orion—is named after a hunter in Greek mythology and can be seen throughout the world. Betelgeuse and Rigel are the brightest stars in this constellation.

   Ursa Major—means "Large Bear" in Latin. This constellation is in the northern hemisphere and contains two of the stars in the Big Dipper, which is used to find the direction north.

   Ursa Minor—means "Small Bear" in Latin. This constellation looks like a small ladle and is part of the Big Dipper, often called the Little Dipper.

   Draco—means "Dragon" in Latin. This constellation is in the far northern sky and is one of the 48 ancient constellations.

   Pegasus—is named after the winged horse Pegasus in Greek mythology. It is located in the northern hemisphere and is one of the 48 ancient constellations.

   Corona Australis (Corona Austrina)— means "Southern Crown" in Latin. This constellation is in the southern celestial hemisphere and is one of the 48 ancient constellations.

Think about This

Constellations were used in ancient times to help navigate ships traveling across the ocean. They also helped keep track of the calendar so people knew when to plant and harvest crops. Like stars, God points you in the way you should go and he is able to guide you each day.

Read Psalm 25:4–5

"Show me your ways, Lord. Teach me your paths. Guide me in your truth and teach me, for you are God my Savior, and my hope is in you all day long."

Learn to Read a Map

Do you ever get lost? Need help with directions? If so, learning to read a map is important. Check out this activity to get you on the right path.

What you need:

A map

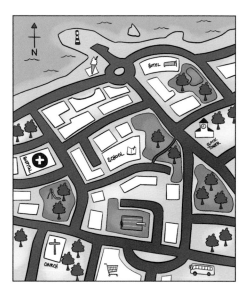

What you do:

1. Get the right type of map. If your family is traveling in the car, you need a road map. If you're hiking on a path near a campsite, you need a topography map. If you are at a theme park, you need a tourist map.

2. Make sure you are looking at the map the correct way, with north at the top and south at the bottom. Look for the direction symbol called the *compass rose*, which shows all four directions: north, south, east, and west.

3. Locate where you are and where you want to go.
4. Most maps have a key of symbols to help you better understand what you're looking at.
5. Look for landmarks, or different locations on the map, and the route you need to take to get where you want to go. There may be more than one route to your destination. You can find the shortest route by looking for the landmarks that are closest to your final destination.

> ### Think about This
> The Bible is like a map because it points you in the direction you should go.

6. Plan your route and enjoy the journey.
7. If you're having trouble reading the map, use a GPS or a location app on a smartphone to get you where you want to go.

Read 2 Timothy 3:16–17

"ALL ScripTure is God-breaThed and is useful for Teaching, rebuking, correcting and Training in righTeousness so That The servanT of God may be Thoroughly equipped for every good work."

Marble Maze

Plan to be a-mazed at the creativity and hand coordination it takes to build and play this marble maze.

What you need:

Cardboard box lid
Construction paper
Marble
Markers
Paper
Pencil
Ruler
Scissors
Straws
Tacky glue

What you do:

1. Find a maze on the Internet or draw the layout of your maze on paper to see if it will work. Here are some helpful hints:
   - Change the lengths of your pathways.
   - Make sure there is one pathway that goes all the way through.
   - All the other pathways lead to dead ends.

- The maze should only have straight lines.
- Make sure a marble can fit easily between the lines.

2. Once you have figured out your maze, draw the layout inside the cardboard lid. Use your ruler to help you measure and create the lines.

3. Cut the straws to fit each line of your maze. Glue in place, creating tunnels, and let dry.

4. Label "start" and "end" using construction paper and markers. This will remind you where to begin and where to end. Glue to your maze. Allow time to dry.

Think about This

Sometimes life feels like being lost in a maze. But just when you think you'll never find your way out, Jesus searches for you and finds you.

5. Play! Place the marble at the start point of your maze. Get the marble from the beginning to the end by holding the base and tilting it to make the marble move. Challenge your friends to beat your time.

Read Luke 19:10

"For The Son of Man came To seek and save The LosT."

Mason Jar Aquarium

It's fun to watch fish zig and zag in between plants and rocks in an aquarium. Create this mason jar aquarium and enjoy it for years to come.

What you need:

Aquarium plant and plastic sea creature from a pet store
Blue food coloring
Blue, silver, or white glitter
Mason jar
Rocks and small seashells
Submersible LED candle
   (optional)

What you do:

1. Fill the bottom of the mason jar with rocks and small seashells.
2. Add an aquarium plant and a plastic sea creature.

3. Mix water and blue food coloring in another container. Add glitter.
4. Pour the mixture into the mason jar, and twist on the lid. Make sure it's on tight!
5. Gently shake the mason jar to see the glitter float around. Make sure you don't dislodge the plants and rocks.
6. At night, add a submersible LED candle for a cool effect.

Think about This

Everything in the ocean and the sky is made by God's hands.

Read Genesis 1:21

"So God created the great creatures of the sea and every living thing with which the water teems and that moves about in it, according to their kinds, and every winged bird according to its kind. And God saw that it was good."

Mason Jar Herb Garden

Have you ever tasted spaghetti with fresh basil and oregano? Help Mom or Dad in the kitchen by planting your own herb garden.

What you need:

Mason jars (quart-sized)
Rocks (or marbles)
Potting mix
Herb plants or seeds—basil, parsley, oregano, rosemary, and mint are great choices
Pencil
Construction paper
Hole punch
Twine
Markers

What you do:

1. Wash the mason jars and rocks (or marbles). Let dry.
2. Add two inches of rocks (or marbles) to the bottom of each mason jar to help the water drain and keep the plants from drowning.
3. Fill each mason jar with potting soil mix. Leave 1–2 inches of room at the top.
4. Place one type of herb into each mason jar.
5. Plant a pinch of seeds into the mason jar by poking holes with the eraser of a pencil and dropping the herb seeds inside. (Follow the directions on the back of the seed packet.) Cover with an inch of potting mix.

> **Think abouT This**
>
> God created plants for us to eat.

6. If you have herb plants, gently pull the roots apart, set in the mason jar, and pack potting mix around the roots and base of the plant.
7. Set on a windowsill that gets 6 hours of sunshine a day.
8. Herbs need to be watered every day or every other day with room temperature water. Keep the soil damp, not soaking wet. Check the seed packet for more detailed instructions.
9. Create fun labels for your herbs so that you remember what you planted in each mason jar. Cut out

three-inch circles from construction paper. Write the name of the herb with markers. Punch a hole in the top of each label. Thread a 10-inch piece of twine through the hole and tie the label around the mason jar.

Read Genesis 1:29

"Then God said, 'I give you every seed-bearing plant on the face of the whole earth and every tree that has fruit with seed in it. They will be yours for food.'"

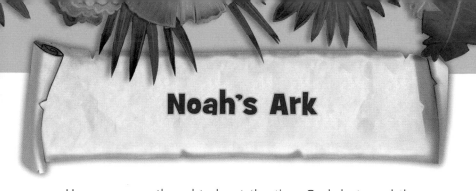

Noah's Ark

Have you ever thought about the time God destroyed the earth with a flood? Build Noah's Ark and remember how God sent a rainbow as a promise never to flood the whole earth again.

What you need:

Cardboard	Markers	Scissors
Construction paper	Craft sticks	Shoebox
Glue	Ruler	Yarn

What you do:

1. Take the lid off the shoebox and set it aside. This will be used later as the base of your ark to add height.
2. With your scissors, cut a door for your ark in the middle of one of the longer sides of the shoebox.
3. Glue a single row of craft sticks to the short sides of the shoebox, careful not to overhang the edges. If using a glue gun, make sure you have a parent present!
4. Glue craft sticks on the longer sides of your shoebox, starting with the bottom layer and working your way up. To create the ark shape, let the end sticks hang off the edge a little bit more each time, starting with the second row.
5. Glue craft sticks around the lid.
6. Glue the shoebox to the top of the lid.
7. Measure the width of the door. Create a ramp by cutting out a rectangular piece of cardboard to fit snugly inside the door you cut. Glue craft sticks to the cardboard.
8. Use glue to attach the end of the ramp to the base of the door.

> ### Think abouT This
>
> **Noah trusted and obeyed God and built an ark 450 feet long and 45 feet high. You, too, can show your love by trusting and obeying God with your life.**

9. Create two of every animal by coloring craft sticks in animal colors, such as pink for pigs, brown for horses, yellow for giraffes, and gray for elephants. Draw on eyes with a black marker. Cut out construction paper ears and noses and glue on your animals. Use yarn for hair.

Read John 14:21

"Whoever has my commands and keeps them is the one who loves me. The one who loves me will be loved by my Father, and I too will love them and show myself to them."

Molding Clay Nature Prints

Do you like collecting things? Here's the perfect opportunity to do what you love and be crafty too.

What you need:

Nature objects

Modeling clay found at a craft store

Acrylic paints

Paintbrush

Mod Podge

What you do:

1. Go outside and collect nature objects, such as pine-cones, twigs, or leaves.
2. With a parent's help, preheat the oven to 275 degrees F.
3. Soften the clay by working it between your hands.

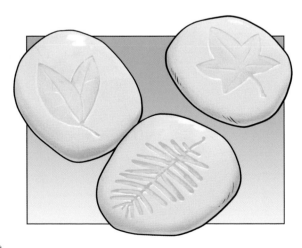

4. Roll the clay into 2-inch balls.
5. Press a ball of clay into a nature object so that the clay is a ¼ to ½ inch thick and there is an impression of the object in the clay.
6. Carefully, peel off the clay.

7. Set on a baking sheet and bake for 20 minutes.
8. Once cool, you can leave the imprints white or paint them. Add a layer of Mod Podge for a glazed look.
9. Optional: To create a necklace or keychain, use a pencil to make a hole in the clay before baking. Add a jump ring and chain once cool.

Read Colossians 1:16

"For in him all things were created: things in heaven and on earth, visible and invisible, whether thrones or powers or rulers or authorities; all things have been created through him and for him."

Obstacle Course

Run, jump, skip, and throw are some of the ways to get your body moving with this activity! Time to get your heart pumping. On your mark, get set, GO!

What you need:

Balls
Beanbags
Boxes
Buckets
Chairs
Chalk
Traffic cones
Frisbees
Horseshoes
Hula-hoops
Jump ropes
Ladder
Old tires
Pool noodles
Sticks
String
2 x 6 lumber

What you do:

1. Set up your obstacle course any way you'd like. Consider these ideas:
   - Place a ladder across two chairs to crawl under, or on the ground to hop through.
   - Using heavy string, hang a hula-hoop from a tree and toss balls through it, or put several hula-hoops on the ground and jump from one to another.
   - Place Frisbees in a pattern on the ground. Toss beanbags on the Frisbees. The farther the Frisbee, the harder it gets!
   - With parent permission, lay the ends of a 2 x 6 piece of lumber on two tires to make a balance beam.
   - Place two buckets a couple of feet apart. Attach the ends of a pool noodle through the handles, and jump over.
   - Crabwalk from one traffic cone to another.
   - Toss a horseshoe at a stake.
   - Run around cones.
   - Make hopscotch with chalk and play.
   - Jump rope.
   - Stack and balance boxes as high as you can.

> ## Think abouT This
>
> **Regular aerobic exercise helps your body get in good shape and gives your heart a workout. When you exercise, you honor God with your body.**

"Do you not know that your bodies are temples of the Holy Spirit, who is in you, whom you have received from God? You are not your own; you were bought at a price. Therefore honor God with your bodies."

Plant a Tree

Trees provide fruit and nuts, shelter for critters, and wood for building and paper. Trees are also beautiful, keep our air clean, and make oxygen for us to breathe. Spring and fall are the best times to plant a tree. Go on! Add a tree to your neighborhood.

What you need:

Tree
Measuring tape
Garden hose
Garden trowel
Plastic tarp
Shovel
Stick
String

What you do:

1. Ask for a parent's permission and help.
2. Choose a spot in your yard to plant the tree that is at

least 15 feet away from the house, power lines, or other trees.

3. Measure the diameter of the tree's roots and soil, called the *root ball*, or how wide it is at the thickest part. Multiply that number by 3 to discover how wide of a hole you should dig. Place the grass and dirt from the hole on a plastic tarp.

4. Uncover the top of the root ball, keeping the burlap sack on as much as possible. Carefully remove the dirt from the top of the root ball so that you can see the top of the individual roots, called the *root flare*.

5. Stand the tree up and measure the height of the tree's root ball. Subtract two inches. This is how deep you need to dig the hole.

6. Dig!

7. Measure the width and depth of the hole you dug. Is it deep enough? Too deep?

Think about This

Tree roots are very important to keep the tree healthy. Having deep roots in Jesus also keeps you healthy and strong.

8. Set the tree in the center of the hole. Position the tree in the direction that looks best to you.

9. If the tree comes with a wire basket or burlap sack, ask a parent to help you cut and remove the covering surrounding the tree's root ball, leaving the bottom in place.

10. Loosen tightly packed soil around the root ball, exposing the tiny roots.

11. Look at the planting directions to see specific soil and fertilizer recommendations for your tree. With a shovel, mix up the soil on the tarp (without the grass) with a shovel, and fill up the hole. Do not cover the root flare!

12. Create a curb of soil around the tree to hold water. Use a garden hose to fill the crater with water. Once the water is absorbed in the dirt, knock down the curb and smooth out the dirt.

13. Spread mulch or wood chips around the entire dirt area leaving 4 to 6 inches around the tree.

14. Water the tree every day for six weeks until the tree roots become established.

Read Colossians 2:6–7

"So then, just as you received Christ Jesus as Lord, continue to live your lives in him, rooted and built up in him, strengthened in the faith as you were taught, and overflowing with thankfulness."

Paper Plate Aquarium

Do you live by the ocean? Have a fish tank? Eat tuna? All three of these things have one thing in common. Fish! Make this paper plate aquarium with as many fish as you like.

What you need:

2 paper plates
Clear plastic wrap
Colored construction
  paper
Scissors
Tape
Stapler
Colored markers
Thread or yarn

What you do:

1. Cut out the center circle of one of the paper plates. Hint: With your scissors, start by poking a hole in the middle of a paper plate to cut out the center circle and keep it looking neat.
2. Cut out a circle of clear plastic wrap larger than the paper plate opening and tape it to the inside of the paper plate.

3. Draw and cut out different types of fish, such as jelly-fish, sharks, starfish, or whales from construction paper.
4. Tape a piece of thread or yarn in different lengths to each fish and attach them to the inside of the paper plate so you can see them through the cut-out.
5. Color an ocean scene on the inside of the other paper plate. Make sure you add colorful coral, plants, and seashells.
6. Staple the plates together. Wiggle your paper plate aquarium back and forth and watch your fish swim!

Think about This

Jesus called his first disciples to be fishers of people instead of fishers of fish.

Read Mark 1:16-18

As Jesus walked beside The Sea of Galilee, he saw Simon and his brother Andrew casting a net into The Lake, for They were fishermen. "Come, follow me," Jesus said, "and I will send you out To fish for people." At once They left Their nets and followed him.

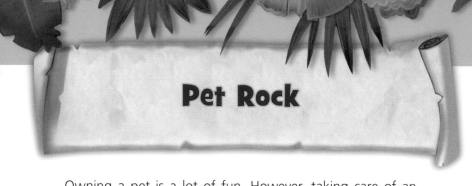

Pet Rock

Owning a pet is a lot of fun. However, taking care of an animal is a lot of work. You need to make sure your pet gets plenty of food, water, and exercise. If you're not ready for such a big responsibility, create this pet rock!

What you need:

Rock
Acrylic paint
Beads
Buttons

Chenille stems
Felt
Small pom-poms
Yarn

Wiggle eyes
Glue

What you do:

1. Go outside and find a rock. Make sure it fits comfortably in the palm of your hand.
2. Wash the rock with soap and water, and allow it to dry.
3. Decide what type of animal you'd like to create. It can be a real animal or one from you imagination.
4. Glue on wiggle eyes.
5. Add a nose using a bead, button, or small pom-pom.
6. Paint a mouth on your pet rock.
7. Cut out ears from colored felt and glue them on.
8. Use chenille stems or yarn to make hair, whiskers, and a tail.
9. Personalize your pet. Be creative!

Think about This

In the beginning, God commanded Adam and Eve to rule over the fish in the sea and the birds in the sky and over every living creature that moves on the ground.

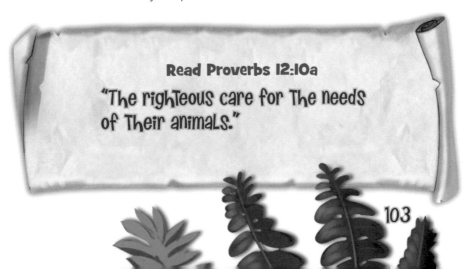

Read Proverbs 12:10a

"The righteous care for the needs of their animals."

Pony Bead Suncatcher

A suncatcher is a decorative piece of see-through material that is hung in a window to bring in and scatter the sun's rays all over the room. Try making this suncatcher from melted pony beads. You will be amazed at how awesome it looks!

What you need:

Pony beads—translucent (see-through) or glitter
Muffin tin or metal cake pan
Grill
Oven mitts
Drill
Ribbon or string

What you do:

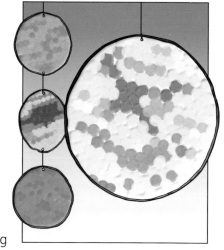

1. Parent involvement required for this project!
   - Warning: Because there may be fumes from melting plastic, it is best to do this activity outdoors on a grill. If you need to do it indoors, preheat the oven to 425 degrees F and turn on the fan and open windows.

- Note: This activity will not ruin pans.
2. Arrange translucent pony beads in a single layer in the muffin tin sections or a metal cake pan. You can create an abstract design or form pictures.
3. Melt on a heated grill for 10 minutes or in the oven for 25 minutes. Before removing from the heat with oven mitts, check to see that the pony beads are melted and appear flat.
4. Once cool, the sun-catchers will pop right out of the muffin tin or metal cake pan when tipped over.
5. Have a parent drill a small hole in each suncatcher.
6. Thread ribbon or string through each hole and hang in a window that gets a lot of light. Enjoy!

Think abouT This

Just as the sun gives us a lot of light, Jesus came to earth to be the light of the world. When you follow him, you will not live in sin and darkness.

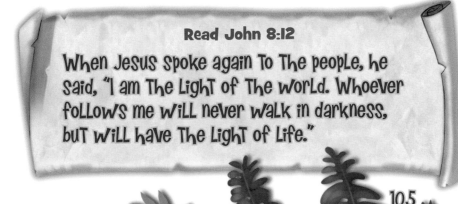

Read John 8:12

When Jesus spoke again To The people, he said, "I am The LighT of The world. Whoever follows me will never walk in darkness, but will have The LighT of Life."

Potato-Art Tote

Design your own tote bag. Collect the following supplies and stamp away.

What you need:

Find an adult to supervise.
  Safety first!
Plain canvas tote
Knife or pumpkin-
  carving tools
Potato
Paper towels
Marker
Fabric paint
Aluminum foil
Newspapers
Recycled cardboard

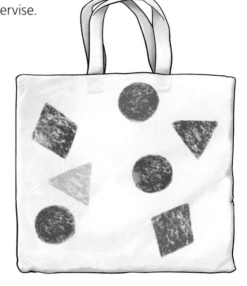

What you do:

1. Cut the potato in half.
2. Place on a paper towel face down and dry the potato as much as possible.
3. Draw a design, such as a geometric shape, with a marker on the flat side of one potato half.

4. Carefully outline the shape by cutting with a knife or pumpkin carving tools.
5. Make slits from the outline of the shape to the outside edge of the potato.
6. Cut around the side of the potato meeting the cuts around the shape.
7. Remove the extra potato sections.
8. Squirt some fabric paint on a piece of aluminum foil.
9. Place your tote on newspaper, and then put a piece of cardboard inside your tote bag so that the paint doesn't seep through to the other side.
10. Dip the potato in fabric paint, being careful not to use too much, then stamp on the tote, using light but firm pressure. Stamp as many times as you wish.
11. Allow the paint to dry.

Think about This

Just as you stamped your design, God marked you with the Holy Spirit when you asked Jesus into your heart.

Read Ephesians 1:13

"And you also were included in Christ when you heard the message of truth, the gospel of your salvation. When you believed, you were marked in him with a seal, the promised Holy Spirit."

Rock Messages

Sending a secret message can bring a smile to someone's face. Make these rock messages to spread joy to others.

What you need:

Acrylic paint

Decorative pens or markers

Paintbrush

Smooth rocks

What you do:

1. Wash the rocks with soapy water, rinse, and dry.
2. Paint one side of the rocks. After they dry, paint the other side.
3. Add an inspirational message, such as *love*, *hope*, *joy*, *peace*, or *be kind* to your rocks with decorative pens or markers.
4. Hide the rocks for others to find.

Think about This

Words can build someone up or tear someone down. You can show God's love to others by encouraging someone today!

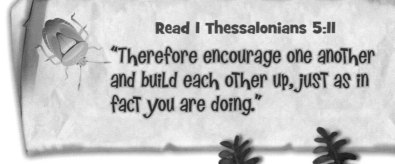

Read I Thessalonians 5:11

"Therefore encourage one another and build each other up, just as in fact you are doing."

Rock Bugs

Are you afraid of bugs? Try making the kind that won't make you scream. Rock bugs!

What you need:

Acrylic craft paint in a
   variety of colors
Black permanent maker
Chenille stems
Newspaper

Markers
Smooth, round rocks
Sponge paintbrushes
Tacky glue
Wiggle eyes

Bee

What you do:

1. Find a smooth rock. Wash with soapy water, rinse, and dry.
2. Spread newspaper on the table.
3. Paint the rock yellow and let dry.
4. With a black marker, draw two thick stripes around the rock.

5. Glue on wiggle eyes.

6. For the wings, cut a Chenille stem in half. Make two loops by wrapping around the tips of your fingers. Glue the wings on the rock bee and let dry.

Caterpillar

What you do:

1. Collect five smooth rocks. Wash with soapy water, rinse, and dry.

2. Spread newspaper on the table.

3. Paint the rocks different colors. Let dry.

4. On one of the rocks, glue wiggle eyes and draw a mouth with a permanent marker. Cut two antennae from a Chenille stem. Glue to the top of the head. Allow time to dry.

5. Add fun designs to the other rocks, like polka dots, stripes, curlicues, zigzags, etc. with markers.

6. Put the caterpillar body together. Place two rocks close together in a row. Glue the head to the first rock. (You might need to prop the head on another rock while it dries.) Glue the remaining rocks to the ones in between. Let dry overnight!

Ladybug

What you do:

1. Collect a smooth rock. Wash with soapy water, rinse, and dry.
2. Spread newspaper on the table.
3. Paint the rock red. Let dry.
4. Color the head using a black marker. Draw a straight black line down the center. Add polka dots on either side.
5. Glue on wiggle eyes. Let dry.

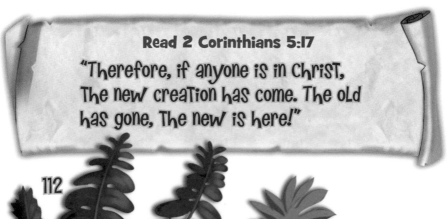

Read 2 Corinthians 5:17

"Therefore, if anyone is in Christ, The new creation has come. The old has gone, The new is here!"

Simple Weaving

Weaving on a cardboard loom is not only fun, but also easy to do. And by the time you're done, you'll have fabric.

What you need:

Masking tape
Piece of cardboard 6" x 8"
Pencil
Plastic needle (optional)
Craft stick
Ruler
Scissors
Yarn

Weaving Glossary

Loom—frame that holds the yarn while weaving.
Warp—evenly spaced, vertical lines of yarn on a loom.
Weave—interlaced thread or yarn to form fabric.
Weft—the horizontal yarn used for weaving.

What you do:

1. To create the *loom*, mark and cut eight evenly spaced slits across the top of the cardboard about a half-inch apart. Do the same thing to the bottom of the cardboard, making sure the slits line up.
2. Tape one end of the yarn to the backside of the cardboard. Make the *warp* by wrapping the yarn around the cardboard, slipping the yarn into the slits you created. Once you finish wrapping, cut and tape the end of the yarn to the backside.
3. Turn the cardboard frame over to the front.
4. Cut pieces of yarn the length of your arm.
5. Tape the end of one piece to a craft stick to use as your needle.
6. To *weave* the yarn, start at the top right corner. Slide the craft stick underneath the first *warp* thread and then over the top of the next thread, and back under the third thread, and so on, all the way to the end. Pull the thread through, but leave a three-inch tail sticking out on the side.
7. For the next row, start on the left side and do the opposite over-under pattern. You are making progress if you don't undo the first row! Pull the thread all the way, but not too tight.
8. After you make a few rows, push up the *weft* yarn so that they are snug against each other.
9. When you have used up the length of your yarn, or if you decide to switch yarn colors, leave a three-inch tail of the color you are currently using. Start the process over with a new piece of yarn, making sure you leave another three-inch tail, and continue the over-under pattern. If you finished the

last yarn by going over, then start the new yarn by going under. If you finished under, then start by going over.

10. Continue weaving until your entire *loom* is full, leaving a three-inch tail of the last *weft* yarn.

11. To take the *weave* off the *loom*, turn the cardboard over. Cut the threads across the center and un-tape the ends. Knot the *warp* ends together in pairs, both top and bottom for a fringed look.

12. You can tape the *weft* yarn tails to the back with masking tape, or thread them through your weaving with a plastic needle.

13. Find a fun purpose for your weaving, such as a coaster for drinks or stick it in a frame as art.

Read Psalm 90:17

"May The favor of The Lord our God rest on us; establish The work of our hands for us—yes, establish The work of our hands."

Sidewalk Tic-Tac-Toe

Tic-tac-toe can be more creative than X's and O's. Try this activity for a new take on the simple game.

What you need:

Acrylic paint

Decorative markers

Paintbrushes

Sidewalk chalk

Smooth rocks

What you do:

1. Wash ten smooth rocks with soapy water, rinse, and dry.
2. For two teams, paint five rocks one color and the other five rocks another color. Allow to dry.
3. Add a design per team, such as hearts versus flowers, or animals versus sports, with decorative markers.

4. Draw a tic-tac-toe board outside on your driveway with sidewalk chalk, making two lines next to each other going down and two across.

Think about This

Whether you win or lose, value others more than the game.

5. To play the game:
   - Each player takes a turn adding a rock to the tic-tac-toe board.
   - First player to get three of their rocks in a row wins!
   - Play as many times as you want.

Read Philippians 2:3–4

"Do nothing out of selfish ambition or vain conceit. Rather, in humility value others above yourselves, not looking to your own interests but each of you to the interests of others."

Sign Language

Fingerspelling is one way to communicate by spelling out words using signs that correspond to each letter of the word. Join millions of people by learning this hands-on language!

What you need:

Your hands

What you do:

1. Learn the sign language alphabet by following the chart below:

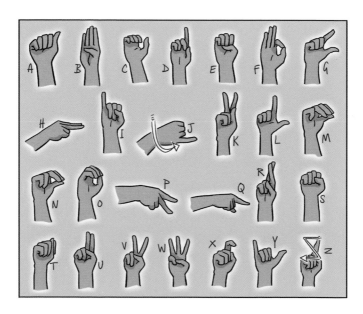

- Can you spell your name using the sign language alphabet? How about the street where you live? Or what you'd like for lunch? Once you know the signs for all the letters, you can spell anything!

Think abouT This
Our hands can be used to communicate as well as serve others.

Read Colossians 3: 23–24

"WhaTeVer you do, work aT iT wiTh aLL your hearT, as working for The Lord, noT for human masTers, since you know ThaT you wiLL receiVe an inheriTance from The Lord as a rewArd. IT is The Lord ChrisT you are serVing."

Slime

Ooey, gooey, and so much fun! A chemical reaction happens right before your eyes with this scientific activity!

What you need:

Cookie sheet
$\frac{1}{3}$-cup school/white glue
$\frac{1}{3}$-cup liquid starch
Food coloring
Paper towels
Plastic bowl
Craft stick

What you do:

1. Using a craft stick, mix together white glue and liquid starch in a plastic bowl.
2. Add a few drops of food coloring and stir. The slime starts to solidify after a few minutes.
3. Squish the slime together with your hands.
4. Remove any extra moisture with paper towels.
5. Play with your slime on a cookie sheet. Roll it, stretch it, and bounce it too!
6. Store the slime in a sealed zipper bag.

Think about This

When you're in a sticky situation, ask God to help you. He will lift you out and set you on a firm foundation.

Read Psalm 40:2

"He lifted me out of the slimy pit, out of the mud and mire; he set my feet on a rock and gave me a firm place to stand."

Solar Oven

Next time the sun is shining and you're hungry for a snack, plan ahead and build this solar oven for a hot treat. You'll be delighted with the delicious result!

What you need:

Aluminum foil
Black construction paper
Clear tape
Empty cereal box
Glue stick
Oven mitts
Plastic wrap

Scissors or utility knife
S'more ingredients:
   chocolate, graham
   crackers, and
   marshmallows
Stick

What you do:

1. Have a parent help you create the oven door by cutting a three-sided flap on the side of the cereal box, leaving an inch border all the way around.
2. Cover the inside of the oven door completely with aluminum foil. Fold around the edges and tape the aluminum foil to the back of the cardboard.
3. Glue or tape black construction paper inside the box.
4. Place your graham cracker squares, marshmallows, and chocolate stacks (s'mores) inside the oven.
5. Wrap a piece of plastic wrap over the opening and tape.
6. Prop the oven door open with a stick and tape it in place to make sure the door stays open.
7. Place your solar oven outside in direct sunlight. Watch the chocolate and marshmallows melt. It will take 30–90 minutes, depending on how hot it is outside.
8. Open the side of the box with oven mitts and place a graham cracker square on each s'more and heat for ten more minutes.
9. Squish and enjoy!

> ### Think about This
>
> Without the sun, there wouldn't be life on earth. Without God's Son, there wouldn't be eternal life in heaven. Praise God for Jesus Christ!

10. Optional: Make other recipes in your solar oven, such as a baked potato, nachos, or roasted apples with cinnamon and sugar.

11. Why this works:
- The sun provides the heat source. Your solar oven can reach up to 200 degrees on a sunny day.
- The foil reflects the sun into the oven.
- The black construction paper absorbs the heat.
- The plastic wrap keeps the heat in.

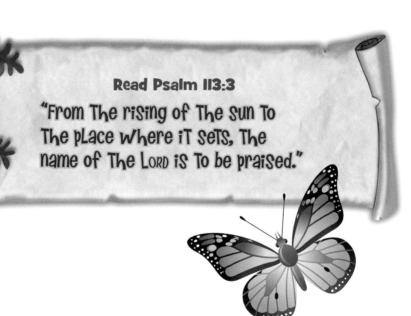

Read Psalm 113:3

"From The rising of The sun To The place where iT seTs, The name of The Lord is To be praised."

Three Survival Knots

Learning to tie different knots is a very important skill for survival. Here are three different knots you can master in no time.

Sheet Bend Knot

What you need:

Thick rope
Thin rope

What you do:

1. Bend the thicker rope into a U, with the opening on the left side.
2. Slip the thinner rope under the bend (or bite) of the U, then over the top thick rope.
3. Slide the thin rope under both the top and bottom of the U so that the thin rope is now pointing down.
4. Tuck the thin rope under itself in the middle of the bend, then bring it over the bend of the thicker rope and tighten by holding on to the thick rope and pulling on both ends of the thin rope.

Think about This

Knots are strong and can create a shelter, a net for fish, or hold a boat in place. You can also be strong because God is with you wherever you go.

Bowline Knot

What you need:

Single length of rope

What you do:

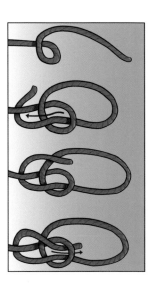

1. Form a loop with the rope so that the right side is on top.
2. Take the tail end of the right side of the rope and pass it through the bottom of the loop. Keep it loose so that there is a larger loop to the right.
3. Pass the end under the remaining rope on the left.
4. Take the end and pass it through the smaller loop, this time from the top.
5. Cinch it closed, using the larger loop to tighten.

Clove Hitch Knot

What you need:

Single length of rope
Post, pole, or something
  to hitch the rope to

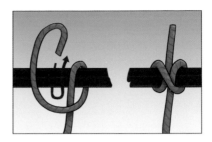

What you do:

1. Loop the rope over a pole. Cross the right side of the rope back over the top, making sure it is to the left of the rope already on the pole.
2. Now bring the end of the rope under the X you just formed.
3. Pull both ends of the rope to tighten the knot.

Read Joshua 1:9

"Have I not commanded you? Be strong and courageous. Do not be afraid; do not be discouraged, for the Lord your God will be with you wherever you go."

T-shirt Bag

Have you outgrown your favorite T-shirt? Turn it into a bag to carry all kinds of things like a beach towel, a ball and mitt, or yummy snacks.

What you need:

Black permanent marker
Large bowl
Old T-shirt
Ruler
Scissors

What you do:

1. Turn the T-shirt inside out.
2. Cut off the sleeves of the T-shirt with your scissors.
3. Lay half of a large round bowl over the collar area, following the curve of the collar but several inches down. Hold the bowl down with one hand, and draw around the edge.
4. Cut around the collar.
5. On the bottom of the T-shirt, measure 1/2 inch intervals and draw 2–inch vertical lines all the way across.

Think abouT This

Transforming an item into something else can take a lot of thought. Being transformed to be more like Christ also starts with your mind. Read your Bible to learn more about how God wants you to think.

6. Make sure the bottom of the T-shirt lines up and cut each line through the front and back of the T-shirt, creating tabs.
7. Tie the front and back tabs together all the way across the T-shirt.
8. Turn the T-shirt outside in.
9. Put stuff in your bag and enjoy!

Read Romans 12:2

"Do noT conform To The paTTern of The world, buT be Transformed by The renewing of your mind. Then you will be able To TesT and approve whaT God's will is—his good, pleasing and perfecT will."

Terrific Tree Swing

Do you have a sturdy tree in your backyard? You're never too old to sit on a tree swing. Grab these items and swing away!

What you need:

100 feet of ⅝" nylon or hollow-core braided
    polypropylene rope
12-inch circular piece of wood from hardware store
Drill with 1 ¼" bit
Spray paint in your
    favorite color
Ruler
Pencil
Sandpaper (120 grit)

What you do:

1. Find the center of
   the wood by making
   an X with a ruler
   and a pencil.
2. Have your parent drill through the
   center of the wood big enough for two pieces of rope
   to fit snugly through.
3. Sand any rough edges.

4. Paint the wood, both sides.

5. To attach the rope to the tree, first fold the rope in half. Put the looped end over the top of the tree branch the swing is going to rest on, and thread the ends through the loop and pull tight so that the rope is snug and secure around the tree.

6. Put the ends of the rope through the hole in the center of the wood and tie a stopper knot. Here's how you do it: Hold both pieces of rope in one hand and wrap it around the top of two fingers. Now wrap the rope four times around your fingers. Gently take the rope off your fingers, keeping it together. Now, take the ends and tuck them through the center (where your fingers used to be), and pull everything tight.

7. Hop on and enjoy the ride!

Think about This

By reading your Bible every day, you will grow strong like a tree with deep roots.

Read Psalm 1:3

"That person is like a tree planted by streams of water, which yields its fruit in season and whose leaf does not wither— whatever they do prospers."

The Perfect Walking Stick

Hiking with a walking stick helps with balance and makes the trek much more fun! Create this one-of-a-kind walking stick for your next big adventure.

What you need:

Stick
Saw (optional)
Pocketknife (optional)
Acrylic paint
Paint brushes
Paper plate
Bowl of water
Paper towels
Mod Podge

What you do:

1. Find a stick that is fairly straight and sturdy, no taller than your shoulder, and a couple of inches thick. Watch out for holes as this could mean there are bugs inside.
2. Stand holding the stick with your arm bent at a comfortable angle and mark the stick 3 inches above your hand so that your parent can trim it with a saw, if needed.

Think about This

Shepherds carry sticks with a hook on the end to lift up sheep that have fallen into a hole or down the side of a cliff. Jesus is called the Good Shepherd because he keeps a watchful eye on his sheep. In fact, he loves you so much that he died on the cross for your sins!

3. Time to decorate your stick! Carve your initials into the wood with a pocketknife (under parent supervision), or paint it any way you like. Squirt a small amount of paint on a paper plate and add stripes or designs. The key is to have fun!

4. Once the paint is dry, seal the stick with a layer of Mod Podge.

5. Go for a walk and enjoy the outdoors.

Read John 10:14–15

Jesus said, "I am the good shepherd; I know my sheep and my sheep know me—just as the Father knows me and I know the Father—and I lay down my life for the sheep."

Tin Can Phone

Fun phone facts:

- A man named Martin Cooper made the first mobile call in 1973.
- In 1983, the cost of the first mobile phone in the US was $4,000.
- A mobile phone has 18 times more bacteria than toilet handles.

Make your own phone and discover how sound travels.

What you need:

Aluminum cans (2)
Duct tape
Felt, glitter, paint, or other decorations
Glue
Hammer
Nail
Scissors
String

What you do:

1. Carefully wash and dry empty aluminum cans.
2. With parent supervision, make a hole in the bottom of each can by hammering a nail through the center.
3. Put duct tape around the edges of the top of the can to protect your ear and mouth from anything sharp.
4. Decorate the outside of each can with felt, glitter, paint, or other decorations.
5. Cut a piece of string up to 10 feet long.
6. Thread the ends of the string through the base of each can and tie a large knot on the inside so it doesn't slip out easily.
7. Hand one phone to a friend and step away from each other until the string is fully stretched apart.
8. Put the phone to your ear and have your friend talk into his can. What do you hear? Now you speak into your can and have your friend listen.

Think about This

God gave you two ears to listen and only one mouth to speak. That means you should listen twice as much as you talk! Take time today to listen to others.

9. How this works:
   - Your friend's voice vibrates inside the tin can, which causes the string to vibrate.
   - Your ear collects the sound vibration, sends them to your brain to process, and then you hear the sound. Cool, huh?

Read James 1:19

"My dear brothers and sisters, take note of this: Everyone should be quick to listen, slow to speak and slow to become angry."

Top-Secret Blanket Fort

If you're stuck inside on a rainy or chilly day, build a fort. Use it as a secret hideout or as home base for a day of play.

What you need:

Blankets
Sheets
Pillowcases
Pillows

Chairs
Heavy books
Clothespins or bag clips

What you do:

1. Find a spot to make your fort, such as your bedroom, the living room, or under the dining room table.
2. Drape a large blanket over the table, a couch, or the edge of your bed to create the roof. Secure it by placing heavy books on the edges, or by tucking the blanket between couch cushions.
3. Set dining room chairs around the outer edge of your fort with the seats facing out.
4. Clip sheets with clothes-pins or bag clips to the sides of your blanket to create the walls, and then drape the sheets over the sides of the chairs.
5. Set books on the seats of the chairs to hold the sheets in place.
6. Fill in any open spaces by clipping on pillow-cases. Use one as your door.
7. Decorate the inside of your fort with rugs, blankets, pillows, and anything else that will make your fort feel cozy.

> ### Think abouT This
> Your blanket fort can be a great place for fun and games, but it can also be a perfect spot to talk to God. Take a few minutes in your comfy, cozy fort to pray.

8. Add a small cardboard box for a table. Bring in snacks and board games.

9. At night, use a flashlight to write in a journal or read a book.

10. Optional: Ask a parent if you can have a sleepover and spend the whole night in your fort.

Read Psalm 32:7

"You are my hiding place; you will protect me from trouble and surround me with songs of deliverance."

Toilet Paper Roll Flowers

Flowers are beautiful and come in a variety of colors, shapes, and sizes. Try making these one-of-a-kind flowers from toilet paper rolls.

What you need:

Acrylic paint
Chenille stems
Green construction
   paper
Glue
Paintbrush
Pencil
Ruler
Scissors
Tissue paper
Toilet paper rolls

What you do:

1. To create the middle of the flower, measure 2 inches down from each end of your toilet paper roll with your ruler, then draw two lines around the toilet paper roll with your pencil.
2. For the petals, draw lines half–inch apart going down

from each end of the toilet paper roll to the center pencil lines you drew.

3. Using your scissors, snip down from the end to the center on each side of the toilet paper roll.
4. Bend back each petal.
5. Paint the flower with acrylic paint. Let dry.
6. Scrunch tissue paper and glue inside the center.

7. Cut out green leaves from construction paper and glue to a chenille stem. Let dry.
8. Glue chenille stem to the flower. Allow time to dry.
9. Place the flower in a pretty vase or give it to a friend.

Read Matthew 6:28-29

"And why do you worry about clothes? See how the flowers of the field grow. They do not labor or spin. Yet I tell you that not even Solomon in all his splendor was dressed like one of these."

Toilet Paper Roll Sheep

Create these toilet paper roll sheep and consider these fun facts:

- Did you know the woolly coat of sheep has been used to make human clothing since the Stone Age? It's true!
- Despite what many people think, sheep are intelligent animals. They are as smart as cattle and are almost as clever as pigs.
- Sheep have large, rectangular pupils, which allow them to have panoramic vision, helping them to see all around themselves and better protect themselves from predators. Cool, huh?

What you need:

Black construction paper
Pencil
Scissors
Cotton balls
4 small sticks
Tacky glue
Toilet paper roll
Wiggle eyes

What you do:

1. Slide two fingers inside the toilet paper roll and put glue all over the cardboard tube, twisting it around as you go.
2. Cover the toilet paper roll with cotton balls. Set aside and let dry.
3. On the backside of construction paper, draw a large oval for the head big enough to fit over the opening of the toilet paper roll. Add ears. Cut out and flip over.

Think about This

God's children are called *his sheep* in the Bible. He loves you and protects you like a shepherd cares for his sheep.

4. Glue on wiggle eyes. Let dry.
5. Put glue around one end of the toilet paper roll. Stick the head on and let dry.
6. Poke sticks through the bottom of the toilet paper roll for legs. (You may need to use the tip of the scissors or pencil to help you create the holes.) Glue in place and let dry.

Read Psalm 100:3

"Know That The Lord is God. It is he who made us, and we are his; we are his people, The sheep of his pasture."

Window Clings

Decorate your window without making a mess! No sticky adhesive on these fun window clings. What are you waiting for? Try this fun activity!

What you need:

Picture to trace
Puffy paint
Wax paper or quart-size plastic zipper bag

What you do:

1. Find a simple object to trace, such as a ball, flower, heart, snowflake, or star from a book, coloring book, or the Internet. Print it out.
2. Lay a piece of wax paper over the top of your picture, or slip the picture inside a plastic zipper bag.
3. Trace the picture using Puffy paint. Make sure all the lines connect and are thick. Let it dry overnight.

> ### Think about This
>
> Just as the window cling grips the window, you are to follow God and cling to him.

4. Gently peel the puffy paint window decal off the wax paper or zipper bag.
5. Warm it up between your hands, then secure the window cling to the glass.

Read Deuteronomy 13:4

"IT is The Lord your God you must follow, and him you must revere. Keep his commands and obey him; serve him and hold fast To him."

Window Picture Tracing

Have you ever wanted to draw like a pro? Here's your chance.
Follow these steps to make a picture-perfect drawing.

What you need:

Blank sheet of paper Picture that you want to
Crayons or markers   trace
Masking tape   Sharpened pencils

What you do:

1. Find a picture to trace from a book, coloring book, the Internet, etc. Print it out.
2. Tape your picture on a window that gets a lot of light.
3. Place your blank sheet of paper on top of your drawing. You should be able to see the drawing through this paper.
4. With your pencil, trace over the lines and details of the drawing while holding the blank piece of paper in place.
5. Re-trace the lines of your drawing with a fine-tipped marker.
6. Color your picture, if you like.
7. Hang your drawing in your room.

Think about This

A good tracing looks like the original picture. When you have a close relationship with Jesus, you will look like him too.

Read Ephesians 5:1–2

"Therefore be imitators of God, as beloved children. And walk in love, as Christ loved us and gave himself up for us, a fragrant offering and sacrifice to God."

Wonderful Wind Chimes

When there is a gentle breeze, wind chimes make their own special tune. Hang one outside your bedroom window and be lulled to sleep by the tinkling sound.

What you need:

Empty aluminum cans in different sizes (5–10 cans)
Acrylic paint in different colors
Paintbrush
Nail
Hammer
Twine
Scissors
10" metal ring from a
    craft store

What you do:

1. Remove the labels and rinse the cans with hot water. Let dry.

2. Paint the cans in different colors. Apply two coats for extra color, then let dry.

3. Add fun designs, such as hearts, stripes, or polka dots.

4. Once you've finished decorating, have a parent help you tap a hole through the center of the bottom of each can with a hammer and nail.

5. Cut different lengths of twine and thread a piece through each can. Make large knots at the end of the twine inside the cans so they can hang.

> ### Think abouT This
> God created you to love and serve him and give him praise!

6. Tie the other end of each piece of twine to the metal ring, spacing them evenly around the circle so that the cans will touch when the wind blows.

7. Wrap twine around the entire steel ring to give it a finished look and to keep the hanging cans in place.

8. To make a hanger, cut three pieces of twine, each about a foot long, and tie them evenly around the steel ring. Knot the ends together at the top making sure it is level.

9. Hang outside and listen for the beautiful sound!

Read Psalm 150

Praise The Lord.
Praise God in his sanctuary;
Praise him in his mighty heavens.
Praise him for his surpassing greatness.
Praise him with the sounding of the
    Trumpet,
Praise him with the harp and lyre,
praise him with the timbrel and dancing,
praise him with the strings and pipe,
praise him with the clash of cymbals,
praise him with resounding cymbals.
Let everything that has breath praise
    the Lord.
Praise the Lord.

Index

Hiking Essentials Pack
Tin Can Phone
Dust pan
Green Camping

E

Elastic bandages
Learn the First Aid Basics
Empty round plastic container
Identifying Animal Tracks
Eraser
Fruit of the Spirit
Extra clothing
Hiking Essentials Pack

F

Fabric paint
Potato-Art Tote
Fall Leaves
Leaf Tracing
Felt
Pet Rock
Tin Can Phone
Fire logs
How to Build a Fire
First-aid supplies
Hiking Essentials Pack
Flashlight
Hiking Essentials Pack
Flour
Identifying Animal Tracks
Flowers
Flower Press
Food coloring
Cloud Soap
Cosmic Art
Mason Jar Aquarium
Slime
Frisbees
Obstacle Course
Fruit
Fruit of the Spirit

G

Garden hose
Plant a Tree
Garden trowel
Plant a Tree
Gauze squares
Learn the First Aid Basics
Glasses
Homemade Rock Candy
Glitter
Mason Jar Aquarium
Tin Can Phone
Glue
Balloon Tennis
Duct Tape Nature Journal
Noah's Ark
Tin Can Phone
Toilet Paper Roll Flowers
Glue stick
Solar Oven
GPS or smartphone
Geocaching
Grill
Pony Bead Suncatcher

H

Half-gallon milk carton
Build Your Own Bird Feeder
Hammer
Tin Can Phone
Wonderful Wind Chimes
Hand broom
Green Camping
Hand towels
Green Camping
Hat
Hiking Essentials Pack
Heavy books
Flower Press
Top-Secret Blanket Fort
Herb plants or seeds—basil,

Tree
Plant a Tree
Tweezers
Learn the First Aid Basics
Twigs
God's Eye
Twine
Build Your Own Bird Feeder
Cross with Sticks and Twine
Duct Tape Nature Journal
Mason Jar Herb Garden
Wonderful Wind Chimes

U

Utility knife
Solar Oven

W

Water
Hiking Essentials Pack
Homemade Rock Candy
Identifying Animal Tracks
Water bottles
Geocaching
Identifying Leaves
Water jug with spigot
Green Camping
Watercolor paints and paintbrush
Coded Secret Message
Waterproof matches
Hiking Essentials Pack
How to Build a Fire
Wax paper
Window Clings
Whistle
Hiking Essentials Pack
White acrylic paint
Bottle Bowling
White construction paper
Coded-Secret Message
White crayon
Coded-Secret Message

White glue
Cosmic Art
Slime
White granulated sugar
Homemade Rock Candy
Whole pecans
Awesome Trail Mix
Wiggle Eyes
Craft Stick and Paper Fish
Pet Rock
Rock Bugs
Toilet Paper Roll Sheep
Wooden spoon or electric mixer
Cloud Soap

Y

Yarn
Build Your Own Bird Feeder
Finger Knitting
God's Eye
Noah's Ark
Paper Plate Aquarium
Pet Rock
Simple Weaving
Your hands
Finger Knitting
Sign Language

Z

Zipper bag
Slime
Window Clings

NIV, Adventure Bible
Hardcover, Full Color

Lawrence O. Richards

Ready for Adventure? Embark on a fun, exciting journey through God's Word with the *NIV Adventure Bible*—now in full color throughout! Along the way you'll meet all types of people, see all sorts of places, and learn all kinds of things about the Bible. Most importantly you'll grow closer in your relationship with God.

Recommended by more Christian schools and churches than any other Bible for kids!

Adventure Bible Book of Devotions, NIV
365 Days of Adventure

Robin Schmitt

Grab your spyglass and compass and set sail for adventure! Like a map that leads to great treasure, this revised edition of the *NIV Adventure Bible Book of Devotions* takes kids on a thrilling, enriching quest. This yearlong devotional is filled with exciting fictional stories about kids finding adventure in the real world. Boys and girls will learn more about God and the Bible, and be inspired to live a life of faith—the greatest adventure of all. Companion to the Adventure Bible, the #1 bestselling Bible for kids.

Available in stores and online!

Visit AdventureBible.com for over 700 free games, activities, and teaching resources.